Yeshua, God's Choice

A Spiritual Journey

By Jeff Kruh

Yeshua, God's Choice
A Spiritual Journey

by Jeff Kruh

First Edition, 2002. Second Edition, 2004.

For additional copies:
website: **www.jeffkruh.com**
toll-free: 1-888-585-3577

ISBN # 0-9720633-2-3

Printed in the United States of America

Yeshua, God's Choice!
A Spiritual Journey

Acknowledgments

This pamphlet is dedicated first to Ha Shem, God of my Jewish people and the God of all people from every nation. I am grateful for every life that God has placed in my path. This pamphlet is also dedicated to those special people, family and friends who have impacted my life in a positive way. Special thanks to my wife Stella for your love, dedication and prayers and for always being there for me. Special acknowledgment and thanks to my parents Ruth and Irving for their sacrifices and love, my wonderful sister Valerie, my father-in-law and mother-in-law Vito and Marie Caputi, brother and sister-in-law Mauro and Joan Caputi. I would also like to thank the I.R.S. for not auditing me this year and Queens Emporium and Quantum Leap restaurants for not putting MSG in my soup. I'm so thankful for so many friends and family that I have been given. You are in my heart as I write this book! Fred and Heidi Farell, Demetrios and Hilda Kastaris, Tom & Cathy Mauro, Ed & Nirit Zagofsky, Rev. Vernon Hodelin, Jerry and Susan Feldman, David and Helene Rosenberg, Stan & Joan Karasick, Barry & Mary Ann Weaver, Vinny Izzo and Roseanne DeAngelis, Ray Vega, Tom

Zivkovich, Donald Sussis, John and Linda Baldino, Austin Wallace Jr., Donald Brownstein and Lisa Tannebaum, Dorothy Falk, Barry and Lasharol Robbins, Ina Perfido, Alice Ruskin, Jaya Egan and Paul Hyman, Geoffrey and Michele Cohen, Vinny Basilicato, David Presler, John and Carol Schiavi, Ann and Manny Cangemie, Gidon and Shira Nelson, Jonathan and Sharon Settel, Helen Weygandt, Dr. DJ Scott, thanks to the mohel who circumcised me for keeping a steady hand, Clemen Sangrado, Joel Weiskopf, Pastor Thomas Bryant, Loris Holland, Warren and Starr Granby, Rabbi Israel Herskovitz, Sol Berkowitz, Rose Kosloff, Ken Simon, Alan and Abbye Binger, Memo and Gail Acevedo, Jack and Kate Jacobs, Jerry and Helayne Weissman, Arkady Kofman, Lee Greene, Baruch Goldstein, David and Carol Hoppe, Robbie Kirshoff, Tyrone and Jarletta Baker, Besai and Jenny Barrera. Special thanks to Nirit Zagofsky, for proofreading the text and Hector Espinoza and Paty Garibay for translating the original English manuscript into Spanish! I'm also truly thankful for you, the reader, for taking time to join me as we share a journey that has resulted in the discovery of a lifetime!

Introduction

Several years ago, the Lord spoke to my heart about writing my story. I am about to share some very personal accounts with you (and I don't mean checking or savings). I am hoping that some of the thoughts and experiences I am about to share will inspire and challenge you to seek God with all of your soul, heart, mind and strength! I also challenge you to pray. God still does hear and answer prayer! Our lives are a gift from God. What we do with them is of the utmost importance to Him. In 1979, I discovered the reality of God's love for me. He does love all people "with an everlasting love" just as the scriptures declare. He has a special and perfect plan for each and every one of our lives and desires that we should be His people and He will be our God.

Twelve years ago, I married Stella, my best friend and the love of my life. At our wedding ceremony, while standing under the *huppah* (wedding canopy), we sang a duet to each other entitled: "Our Love, Filled with God's Love." The lyrics follow: "Our love, filled with God's love is unending. Our love is a song that's just begun. And following His plan, for this woman and this man, there's just no end to our love!" The Lord gave us this special song. God has a special song for you, if you will listen for it. He composed it especially for you. If you desire Him, He will sing His love song to your heart! Not only will you hear the melody, but you yourself will blend with God's harmony! God's music is all about Him. He is the music! I can rejoice with the words of the "sweet psalmist of Israel," King David who said: "The Lord is my strength and song and He has become my salvation." (Psalm 118:14) I am eternally grateful to Ha Shem for choosing me and allowing me to personally experience His love, forgiveness, joy, power, deliverance and "the peace of God, which surpasses all human understanding!" God has proven to me conclusively, beyond any shadow of a doubt, that Yeshua (Jesus) is the promised Jewish Messiah. I can say together with Rabbi Saul of Tarsus, "For I am not ashamed of the Good News, since it is God's powerful means of bringing salvation to everyone who keeps on trusting, to the Jew especially, but equally to the gentile." (Romans 1:16)* It is God's cry at this very hour that His chosen people, the Jews, and all people might discover that Yeshua is indeed God's choice for us all!

*Scripture quotation is taken from the Jewish New Testament, c 1979 by David H. Stern and used with permission of Jewish New Testament Publications Inc., P.O Box 615, Clarksville, Maryland 21029. Available through Messianic Jewish Resources. www.messianicjewish.net.

> **"To everything there is a season,**
> **A time for every purpose under heaven.**
> **A time to be born......" Ecclesiastes 3:1,2**

My time had come. I entered the scene on April 24, 1948 at 3:20 PM, an appointment that I unknowingly had been destined for. I was a bright, bouncing baby, ready to boogie!

When I opened my eyes, I was in the Bronx, New York City. God had given me two wonderful parents, Ruth and Irving, to care for me. My new home was 3435 Olinville Avenue, a small apartment in a six floor tenement located by Bronx Park (A place that Ralph Kramden and Ed Norton would probably feel very much at home to live in).

At a very early age my parents recognized that I had a musical gift so I began to study piano with Remo Preziosi, the father of my two closest compatriots, Louis and Raymond. Louis and Raymond lived upstairs on the fifth floor, and we lived on the ground floor. Remo's wife, Rose, was a fabulous cook, and I was privileged to eat spaghetti and meatballs there on many occasions. They would come downstairs for matzoh- ball soup and lambchops, mashed potatoes and creamed spinach. We would stuff ourselves in front of the television watching *The Abbot and Costello Show*, *Popeye the Sailor*, *The Three Stooges*, *Terrytoon Circus* and, of course, *Superman*. I once tried to emulate Superman and ran across a room, took a flying leap and hit my head on a hard part of the couch. I discovered the law of gravity the hard way. After studying piano with Remo for about one year, my parents decided that I should apply for admission to the Juilliard School of Music in Manhattan. At my entrance audition I sang "The Witchdoctor" and accompanied myself on the piano. I played several songs by ear and was evaluated by several jurors. Juilliard soon informed me that I was accepted as a piano major and given a scholarship. I was granted a scholarship for seven consecutive years (which was necessary because of our low family income). Dad was always working two and three jobs to support us, and I was always happy when we could spend some quality time together. Mom was busy cooking, cleaning and doing chores to make us comfortable.

We lived next to a large lot where we would engage in activities such as "dirt-bomb wars" (throwing pieces of hardened earth at each other) and looking for and capturing various types of insects. I was a very curious child, as most children are, and loved exploring. Adjacent to the other side of the lot was a local synagogue with a fairly large school yard. Here we would play punchball and stickball and other group games such as "hide and seek," that were "politically correct."

In 1955, my sister Valerie was born. I was thrilled to have a sister to play with. She had golden hair loaded with curls. (I placed notes under many of my neighbors' doors, heralding her arrival!) I was seven years old when Valerie was born.

The Chicken or The Egg?

"Which came first, the chicken or the egg?" Sounds familiar? As a child, I attempted to come up with an answer to this question with no success. With fervent intensity, I would try to understand the origin of creation. Where, when, how and why did it all begin? I would go through a mental visualization process of removing things until I was left with air, space and color. Then I would ponder, again and again, what was the first thing there ever was, and how was it created? Did the earth and universe come into existence by a random series of events? Did people evolve from lower life forms into a higher one? Is " **evil**-ution" a rational and cohesive theory that is reliable and can be proven scientifically? Is there a living God whom I can know personally? What is truth? Could there be a design without a Creator-designer? I was determined to find the answers. I remember as a young child, seeing a visual mental image of a male figure standing and holding a Bible,(who it was, I don't know; whether or not it was a dream or a vision, I can't recall). Today, I see this was a prophetic event. God was always working in my life. Ultimately, all my questions about God, truth and the meaning of life, as well as what is the significance of being born Jewish, were to be found in the

Bible (the *Tanakh** and the New Covenant scriptures.)

Today I am certain that my spiritual journey in search of the truth was orchestrated by the grace and goodness of God! I know that God made me with an emptiness in my heart that could only be filled by the Ruach Elohim (The Spirit of God). For years, I tried to fill this spiritual vacuum with other things to no avail. I was going to find the truth somehow, some way! While attending PS #41 in the Bronx, I wrote:

"A Child's Prayer"
I thank you God for a hundred things,
For the flower that blooms,
for the bird that sings,
for the sun that shines,
and the rain that drops,
for ice cream and raisins and lollipops.

Amen.

I can't forget the prayer that my mother recited daily in my presence: "Blessed art thou O Lord our God, King of the universe whose glorious kingdom is forever and ever. Thank you for taking care of mom and dad and Jeff and Valerie and continue to take care of mom and dad and Jeff and Valerie. Amen." God has been faithful in answering this prayer!

As a boy growing up in the 50's, I knew that I was Jewish and that the Jews are God's chosen people. Our family would celebrate the Jewish holidays together (Passover, Rosh Hashanah, Yom Kippur, and Chanukah). In addition, on Christmas Eve, my parents always put up a Christmas tree in the living room, nicely decorated, with one or more empty stockings hanging up soon to be filled with all kinds of surprises. When I woke up on Christmas day, the living room

---

*comprised of *Torah* (The Five Books of Moses), the writings, and the prophets the *Tanakh* is also known as the Old Testament.

floor was covered with many gifts. What a score!!! I often wondered how Santa could come down the chimney since we didn't have one. Perhaps he would come through a window or the front door. Could it be that this was an "inside" job? When I asked my parents how I arrived here on earth, my mom said that a stork brought me. How did he know my address? I couldn't accept this and ultimately concluded that this explanation was for the birds! I was a very curious kid. One day I went to the refrigerator, took out an egg, walked over to the sofa with it and sat on it hoping to birth a little "chicklet. " I got scrambled eggs instead. What a letdown! I was determined to find the answers to life's most important questions!

My Introduction to Gambling

At the age of eleven, our family moved to Queens, New York, to the town of Briarwood where I was enrolled at Van Wyck J.H.S. #217. I maintained a very small circle of friends during those days. My time was spent mostly practicing the piano, reading, doing homework and school studies and watching TV. One day a classmate named Donald, told me about betting the horses and invited me to Aqueduct racetrack in Ozone Park, Queens, N.Y. I was, perhaps, twelve years of age at the time. I accepted the invitation, not knowing or comprehending that this seemingly harmless visit to the track would open the door wide to years of misery, despair and an addiction to gambling which would attempt to destroy my life!

There is a spiritual truth that talks about the sins of past generations being inherited by succeeding generations. The "sins of the fathers" do visit their children and they replicate that very same behavior. I am thankful that, with the exception of an occasional card game, my dad was not a gambler. Notwithstanding, gambling was nothing new to our family. My dad's brothers were heavy gamblers. One brother eventually committed suicide. My dad's other brother was known to take bets on horses. My mom's brother was a compulsive gambler and lost big bucks at the racetrack. He would go to the $100 betting windows, where I would see him place large wagers. He would teach me about handicapping the horses, interpreting the racing form and being a "smart" bettor. I would now be following in his footsteps. I never dreamed that I would be lying, cheating and stealing from family and friends to accommodate this miserable "sport of kings." For approximately the next 18 years, from junior high school through high school, college years and beyond, most of the money I earned was used in gambling mainly on horses and card games. I could never save any money. I had to bet. I lost thousands of dollars, whatever I could earn or steal to support my addiction. I remember having a talk with a good friend of mine named Stan. We were sitting in his car, and he told me that I had to stop gambling and that it was ruining my life. He said it would surely destroy my life, career, family relationships and friendships. I knew he was right. I wanted to stop, but I knew that this would be impossible. At this time I didn't know that with God, **all things are possible!** I went to a Gambler's Anonymous meeting and quickly found that it wasn't for me. At GA, they believe that compulsive gambling is a disease that can be arrested but never cured. Even if I attended the meetings, I would always be a compulsive gambler. I would have to faithfully attend the meetings and join the program, relying on group support and phone chains to keep me from betting, one day at a time. Nevertheless, I would still be tormented with an insatiable desire to bet. I knew that I would go nuts if I could not bet. I considered GA a cosmetic approach to my problem. If I could find a cure for compulsive gambling, I would go for it. Thank God that I did!!! I will discuss some insights concerning compulsive gambling and how to be totally set free from this addiction a little later in this booklet.

Early Religious Training - Where is God?

At the age of twelve I began studying for my up and coming Bar Mitzvah the following year. My rabbi was Israel Herskovitz. He was an orthodox jew. He would visit our home weekly and teach me to read Hebrew and recite prayers, and taught me my Torah and Haftorah portions for the Bar Mitzvah. At age thirteen, I was to become a "son of the law." According to the rabbis, I would become a "man" and now fully accountable to God for my actions. In reality I acted more like a "son of a gun" than a "son of the law."

I became a Bar Mitzvah at a local conservative Jewish *shul* in Jamaica, New York. I received a certificate of Bar Mitzvah and my parents gave me a beautiful reception and celebration at Burbaran's Restaurant in Queens. In my heart, I still had many serious, unanswered questions. How can I have a living personal relationship with the living God? What is spiritual truth? How can I know God personally? Where might I find Him? In God's love and wisdom, He let me feel this void for His presence in my life. The answer was coming, but it would take many more years to arrive.

Some months passed since my Bar Mitzvah, and I decided that the logical place for a Jew to find God was the synagogue. I decided to attend weekly Shabbat services at Young Israel of Briarwood, a local orthodox congregation. Some months went by, and I concluded that the reality, presence and power of God was not available through that venue. I received no knowledge or revelation of God and knew that I was the same person. Knowing God personally would surely result in a transformation of my life and would also yield the fruit of a true and genuine "shalom" (peace) which I wanted so very much.

The Journey Continues

I remember walking down a street with my friend Pete and asking him if he believed in God. His response was, "God? There is no God." Could Pete be right? When I further pondered this question, God intervened in a personal way, and He settled it for me once and for all! I started to feel very physically ill with an upset stomach. The thought of atheism began to nauseate me, and I knew intuitively that somehow God exists. All of my life, there was a "still small voice" speaking to me and working in me, always bringing me closer to a face-to-face encounter with the living God of Israel!

I had a very good Jewish friend named Abbey who also was a musician. Abbey was a buddhist. He convinced me to attend services and teachings at the zen "temple of enlightenment" in the Bronx. Abbey believed that following the teachings of Buddha is the right and true spiritual path that leads to enlightenment. I attended services for several months and bowed before a lifeless man-made idol and a "false god." I had never read Psalm 115, written by King David: "Not unto us, O Lord, not unto us, but to Your name give glory, because of Your mercy, because of Your truth. Why should the Gentiles say, so where is now their God? But our God is in heaven: He does whatever He pleases. Their idols are silver and gold, the work of men's hands. They have mouths but they do not speak: eyes they have but they do not see: They have ears, but they do not hear: noses they have but they do not smell: they have hands, but they do not handle: feet they have, but they do not walk: nor do they mutter through their throat. Those who make them are like them: so is every one who trusts in them. O Israel, trust in the Lord: He is their help and their shield."

One day Abbey and I were eating food in our favorite Indian restaurant in the East Village (The Shah Bagh on East 6ᵗʰ Street). In addition to eating hot and spicy Indian food, we would walk down the street to our favorite dealer and score some marijuana. Our lives were going up in smoke but we didn't know better. Our conversation was focused on issues of life and spiritual matters. I made a comment that the most important thing in life is to love one another. Abbey responded to this by saying "there is no love." What he meant by this, I'm not certain, but it had the result of my rejecting buddhism as a false religion and continuing on my search for God and truth. I firmly believed that when I found the "truth," whatever that might be, it would be the truth for all. One God and one truth for all mankind. Truth has to be absolute not relative. I found statements like, "It may be truth to you, but it's not truth for me," to be unacceptable and contradictory, distorting the very intended meaning of the word "truth." I also knew intuitively that when the truth was revealed to me, love would be a foundational expression of that truth. It would also demonstrate love in its purest and highest form.

After my brief investigation of buddhism, I went to New Hampshire to visit an Indian guru, a so-called "ascended master." This was really an expression of a Hindu occult religion. Their false teaching went something like this. After receiving initiation by the "master," he would accept your "bad karma," and you would not have to return to earth for more than three incarnations. He was to be worshipped as God, and you would be his disciple. Finally, you would wind up in "satch kand," which would be the equivalent to heaven. (You really wind up in the "other" place.) The guru and other ascended masters had "charged names." They were charged with occult power released by Satan and his emissaries. Posing as "angels of light," they were being used by the devil to stop people from knowing, loving and serving the one true God of Israel, the God of Abraham, Isaac and Jacob, and His Messiah Yeshua (Jesus), the light of the world! I decided that I would receive initiation into this cult several months later.

The weekend of my "initiation" was finally approaching, and I was planning to drive to New Hampshire, but something unexpected happened. I became very ill with some sort of virus and had to cancel my plans. I didn't realize that God was intervening once again in my life! He remembered the cry of my heart to find Him, and God was now removing another obstacle out of my way. He was shutting the door to the Hindu occult religion and following gurus. (Although I was certainly involved in the spirit realm of the demonic, and the powers of darkness were still working overtime in a futile attempt to thwart God's plans for my life, God would battle my enemy, Satan, and ultimately be victorious. Baruch HaShem!!) Weeks and months passed, and my desire to be initiated waned cold. I was losing interest quickly. I was now beginning to have serious doubts as to whether or not this was the true and right path that God would have me take. One day while driving in my car, I began to meditate on the "charged name" of this so-called master. I kept repeating his name in my mind when another thought came to mind: "what's wrong with meditating on Christ?" I decided that I would now do an "equal time" comparative study. I would focus and meditate on the false master's charged name and then Yeshua the Messiah to see if there was a difference or if something would happen. When I meditated on the charged name of the "false Christ," absolutely nothing happened. However, when I meditated and called out to Yeshua, who is the true Messiah (Christ), God filled me with a sense of His presence, power and love, God was trying to tell me that I could trust in Him and that Yeshua is indeed my Messiah. God was right there, again guiding me in the right direction. He never changes! I decided that if I was given the choice to follow anyone, it would be Yeshua, not Satan's demonic emissary! This was the end of my desire to be involved in the Hindu occult! At this point, however, I was not very anxious to follow this special seed that my Heavenly Father graciously dropped into my heart, but the Lord was to water this seed until the day when I became a true believer and follower of Messiah Yeshua. God was lovingly beginning to reveal to me that Yeshua was the truth that I'd been longing for and through Him I could know God personally. God was going to continue to use circumstances and people in my life to draw me into His loving arms!

Groping through Spiritual Darkness

During my teenage years and throughout my twenties and early thirties, I experienced what I considered to be psychic phenomenon or ESP experiences. As I reflect on these events and occurrences, I understand today that there was a real battle being fought for my soul between God and Satan and his demonic hosts. The battle still rages on even now as I write this pamphlet, but God has given me the victory through Messiah Yeshua! God speaks to people today and so do demon spirits. The voice that would tell me of something to happen in the future, that would save my life or protect me was God's Ruach Elohim (Holy Spirit). Likewise, the voice telling me lies, enticing me to ignore my conscience, live in open rebellion towards God and His commandments, exhibit all sorts of destructive behavior (such as gambling and substance abuse) and continue to live in sin (thereby forfeiting eternal life with God), was Satan and his demon spirits. Years ago, my wife Stella worked in a bank as a bank teller. She told me that the tellers were taught how to recognize counterfeit bills by studying the genuine bills, not the counterfeit ones. Likewise, there are many false doctrines, religions and cults out there. Only when an individual is sealed with God's Holy Spirit, will one have the ability to recognize any and all counterfeit spirits that are in operation in the spirit realm.

I was always interested in the supernatural. As a child I watched plenty of horror and monster movies. In my late teens, I began smoking pot, tried cocaine and was addicted to valium for some time. The use of drugs opens up an individual to the spirit world and realms of the demonic. I became fascinated with ESP (extra-sensory perception). I attended a seminar that tried to develop this so- called "gift." Later I learned that just because an individual experiences something powerful in the spirit realm doesn't mean that it comes from God. In the Bible, when Moses stood before Pharoah and his magicians, Aaron threw down his staff, and it became a serpent; the magicians and the sorcerers threw down their rods, and they also became serpents, but Aaron's serpent swallowed up the magicians' serpents. God was behind Moses and Aaron, but Satan was empowering the rods of Pharoah's magicians and sorcerers. It is also noteworthy to mention that in the *Tanakh*, God says that mediums, spiritists, necromancers and witches were to receive the death penalty. These are crimes against a Holy God which required divine justice. Astrology was another "art" I dabbled in. I went to two professional astrologists to get my chart and private readings. Astrology is also condemned by God in the Scriptures. In order to find God's plan for your life, you need a Bible, not an ephemeris!*

God's Timing

While I was attending Jamaica High School in Jamaica, New York, one morning I went into a candy store on the corner of 168th Street and Hillside Avenue. I went to the shelf, selected some candy then went to the back of the line to pay for it as there were maybe five people in front of me. Suddenly, I heard this voice from within telling me to leave the store at once. At first I fought it, dismissing this as an illogical and unacceptable impulse. I wanted my candy; there was no reason to leave the store before I completed my purchase. The urge to leave the store became stronger

---

*(astronomical almanac used by astrologists)

and stronger, then overpowering. I quickly left the store, but the voice said "go faster, walk faster." Less than a minute went by, and I heard a loud sound. I stopped and turned around to notice that there must have been some sort of accident or explosion. I went back towards the candy store where I saw a woman sprawled on the sidewalk. A car had gone out of control, going up onto the sidewalk and crashing into the liquor store, which was right next to the candy store I had been in just moments before. Reports said there were multiple injuries, and people were injured by flying glass, I believe that God called me out of the candy store to avoid injury or death.

"I once met a bull in Bullville"

One night during the early 1970's, I was driving home from a piano lounge gig I had just finished playing in Middletown, New York. I was driving down Rt. 302 North through the town of Bullville, New York, This was a dark winding road with fields and farm acreage to my right and left. It was a two-lane road separated by a double line, each lane going in the opposite direction. Suddenly, I saw as clear as day, a vision of a black bull in front of me. I knew that I would soon be meeting this unwanted visitor. I knew that I was going to crash into this animal at any time now. I became frightened and wondered what I should do, maybe stop the vehicle, but there wasn't any place to pull over. I kept driving. My driving speed was approximately 25m.p.h. Suddenly, a tremendous sense of peace flooded my soul, and, at the same time, a voice spoke to my mind and my spirit saying; "Relax, you are about to hit the animal you just saw in the vision. Keep both hands firmly gripping the wheel. You will not be injured." I was transformed from a state of panic to total assurance. I knew when this voice spoke, it was truth speaking to me. Maybe 15 seconds elapsed and suddenly, the same black bull that I had seen in the vision stepped in front of me, turning his head towards me. I slammed into his neck, and head. The impact cracked my windshield, but it remained intact. There was some body damage to the grille and front of my car. Blood was on the windshield. On the hood of the car was a hole in the form of a scoop, which went right through the metal. I believe this was a result of the animal's horn making contact with the hood of my car. He had left his insignia, a reminder and witness to me that I had entered into a supernatural realm that I did not fully comprehend, one in which I needed to continue to search for spiritual truth. I escaped this accident without injury. In those days, I relegated this occurrence to "psychic phenomena." Today I know that this was God, once again intervening on my behalf, sparing me from harm and drawing me to Himself!

Demonic Possession

The seventies were turbulent times for me. I continued in my destructive lifestyle. I would take actions without considering or caring about the consequences. My gambling was completely out of control; my sexual appetite and lust were insatiable. I always enjoyed getting high but inside I was still empty, still searching. I was a perfectionist "par excellence." I was looking for perfection in myself, in others, in situations and relationships. God was trying to tell me, "You don't have to be perfect. In fact that is impossible and unrealistic. I am perfect. Don't put all your faith in imperfect people. You will surely be disappointed. Put all of your faith, trust and hope in me! Stop trying to be something that you can't be!" It was some time in my twenties that the Lord revealed to me that if I didn't find "the truth," there would be more suicide, destruction and generational curses continuing to be perpetuated in my family. There were many times that I could feel a very strong presence of evil and demonic spirits. God was teaching me the spiritual principle that "the wages of sin is death!" Continued open rebellion to

God's commandments was resulting in Satan and his demons having more authority in my life. Many people don't believe that the devil exists, but he is a real entity nevertheless, having access to our thoughts, minds, and lives. The *Tanakh* and the New Covenant scriptures verify the reality of Satan and demonic powers. Thankfully, Satan is subject to God's authority.

The following frightful incident happened when I was in my mid-twenties, living in Manhattan. One night I was relaxing, lying on a couch, when suddenly I was thrown off of the couch by a very powerful force. I was about to experience something terrifying! I was filled with a demon spirit (or spirits). They (or he, or it) started to speak, using my vocal cords in another voice which was not my own. It was a hideous voice coming from the very pit of hell. I could feel the presence of powerful demonic spirits all around me and in me. I just had a small part of my own mind and will in operation. I remember yelling out "why me?" These demons were yelling and screaming at me to run full force through the large glass window in front of me. Furthermore, I was being pulled by these powers of darkness to obey them. Satan wanted to kill me on the spot before I knew Messiah, so that I would spend an eternity in the presence of Satan and his demons instead of in the presence of my Savior and my God, the only true and living God, the God of Israel and all nations and peoples. Satan was trying to force me to commit suicide. (I will mention here that I was not suicidal at this or any other time of my life. I was fighting these demons on my own strength with everything that was left in me. I surely would have lost this life-and-death battle if God hadn't been fighting on my behalf). I managed to turn my body in the opposite direction and ran towards the door. The demon spirits were trying to tear me apart. They were yelling "jump up, jump up" and were trying to get me to open the door and jump or leap without looking. Directly in front of the door was a long stone staircase. I could have suffered bodily injury or death if the door had opened. God had another plan. The door jammed; I couldn't turn the knob. I felt as though I had huge physical strength yet the door would not open. Suddenly, I felt the demonic presence leave me, and I was restored to my right mind. Yeshua cast out the demons! I turned the doorknob (it now opened easily), and I walked out of the apartment, down the staircase and onto the street. I was scared out of my wits. Why did this happen to me? I wasn't high on drugs. I know that a demon spirit or spirits entered my body. But why? I would find the answer one day. Thank God, He was always there to protect me and not let me die without knowing Him and receiving His salvation through Messiah Yeshua. My major concern was making sure that this would never happen to me again. Where or to whom would I turn next? I knew that I had experienced demonic possession. I knew that a psychiatrist would interpret my experience as acute psychosis and schizophrenia. I knew that the spirit world was real, and that I had tapped into a supernatural realm. I also now knew beyond any shadow of a doubt that the devil was real and was trying to destroy me. The Bible has an abundance of scriptures and teaching about Satan, demons and the powers of darkness. It also has examples of people who were demon possessed and Messiah Yeshua casting the demons out of them. Taking medication would not be the right move. (You can't medicate the devil. He must be cast out by God Himself!) Today I know that Messiah commanded the demons to get out of my body, just as He had done in the Bible. Baruch HaShem! Praise the Lord!! Today I know that the good news of Messiah Yeshua "is the power of God that leads to salvation to anyone who believes, to the **Jew first,** and also to the gentile." (Romans 1:16) What a wonderful, merciful, compassionate and forgiving, loving, righteous and just God there is to know, love and serve!!! Some of you reading this right now might be thinking, "I'm glad this worked for you. Your life was a mess and you needed something; I don't need to believe this stuff." If you're thinking this way, you've come to the wrong conclusion. The same Satan who tried to destroy me is also your enemy and he's going after you!

My next move was to call a friend of mine who was involved in "white" magic and witchcraft. I was hoping that she could advise me as to what I could do to protect myself from any future attacks of the devil. She suggested that I do certain enchantments and incantations and light candles to ward off any curses against me or attacks from Satan in the future. I did not, however, take her advice because I felt that this would open up an even deeper involvement in the occult than I could handle. I intuitively felt that witchcraft was not the way to battle and ultimately defeat Satan in my life. I felt that it was better for me to find my answers elsewhere.

College Days

In 1964, I entered Queens College (located in Flushing, Queens, New York) as a Liberal Arts degree candidate. After receiving my Associate of Arts degree, I entered the music program and graduated Queens College with a B.A. degree in Music in February 1972. After graduation, I would return to the practice rooms in the music building to practice piano and hang out with friends. I enrolled in graduate and undergraduate courses in music and Jewish religious studies. Queens College was a special place for me. I liked being in that environment, learning and also meeting people, especially musicians.

In my late twenties, while at Queens College, I met a very talented musician named Loris. We would hang out together, play duets together on the piano, smoke pot and talk about spiritual matters. He began to share with me that He goes to "the church of the living God." He told me that Yeshua the Messiah(Jesus Christ) was Lord and that soon He would give his life to God and be "saved." I felt that what Loris was saying might be true and that it certainly was, at the very least, worth investigating. I met another musician named Warren who would share spiritual insights from the scriptures, which demonstrated the truth of the gospel of Messiah Yeshua. Warren attended the same church that Loris did. I visited their small Pentecostal church in South Jamaica named Rescue Church of Christ of the Apostolic Faith. The first time I walked into the church, I could sense that God was present there. People had genuine love for me and for each other and certainly for God. I began to read the Bible, listen to sermons and hear other believers share what God had done for them personally. In addition, I discovered that these people claimed to know the God of Israel personally, and that I could know Him, too, if I believed that Jesus was my Messiah and received Him into my heart and life as Lord and Savior. This was quite a challenge, having been brought up as a Jew. I always ignorantly understood that belief in Jesus was belief in a foreign god. I certainly was turned off to statues, worshipping saints and angels, confessing to priests, praying to Mary etc. None of these practices are found in the Bible and are contrary to the Word of God. When I began to read the Bible for myself, I slowly began to discover that, in fact, Yeshua was a Jew, and if He was the Messiah, it would not betray my Jewishness to believe in Him and follow His teachings. The more I read the scriptures, the more I could see that Yeshua probably was my Messiah and the Savior of the world. God was continuing to use people and events in my life to lead me to the truth of the gospel!

1977-1978

It was during this time that I decided to take a step of faith and be immersed in water in the name of Yeshua. I really felt God drawing me to make a commitment, and that this was the right course of action to take. That soft, gentle voice that I knew to be the voice of the Lord was now speaking to me out of the scriptures, and assuring me that Yeshua is, in fact, who He says He is, "the way, the truth and the life."(John 14:6) However, I didn't make a true commitment, and I didn't fully repent. Satan was about to launch another all-out assault on my life. In the tenth chapter of John, Yeshua calls Satan a thief. In verse 10 Yeshua says: "The thief does not come except to steal, and to kill, and to destroy. I have come that they may have life, and that they may have it more abundantly."

It was now November 1978, and Thanksgiving soon would arrive. Because I had not yet come to know the Lord and my heart wasn't right, I had given Satan further authority in my life. Satan was desperately trying to stop me from getting saved and knowing the "truth that would set me free." (John 8:32) However, God had predestined me to know, love, serve and worship Him in "spirit and in truth" (John 4:24) even "from the foundation of the world" (Ephesians 1:4) as the scripture plainly states.

During this time Satan again tried to kill me. He had me running down the road and in the path of oncoming traffic. I was experiencing my final bout with demonic possession. A state police car pulled up to me, a police officer jumped me, put me in handcuffs and off I went to the "looney house." (The policeman's name was Patrolman Love. He stopped me from getting hit by a car but it was God's love for me that sent Patrolman Love to remove me from harm's way.) I was taken to a state hospital and medicated. Within about a week, I was moved to another hospital for a stay of about one month. During my stay I knew that I needed spiritual counseling and that my ultimate hope for deliverance would come from God. My mom had given me the number of a rabbi, and I also had the telephone number of Elder Hodelin, the pastor of Recue Church. I prayed and asked God to lead me to the one from whom I would receive spiritual guidance. When I called the rabbi, he seemed totally disinterested and said that he was too busy and couldn't help me. When I called Elder Hodelin and told him about my current situation, he and his wife quickly came to the hospital to see me. Their love, concern and support for me was a source of comfort and strength that I will surely never forget. Shortly after their visit, I was discharged from the hospital and went to live in my parents' home for a short season to fully recuperate. God graciously restored my mind, and I was seriously trying to understand all of the implications of what had just occurred, as well as reflecting on what God would have me do. I asked God if I would ever have the faith to know Him and the heart to serve Him. Soon after, the Lord spoke to my heart and assured me that I would! God's love and mercy knows no bounds!

Bon Voyage!

It was now spring of 1979, and I landed a gig in the Carribean (on the isle of St. Maarten) as a pianist in one of the island's major hotels. I quickly resumed my decadent lifestyle of drinking, smoking pot, womanizing, and, of course, I could be found in the casino every night. I had plans of working in the hotel until I could save enough money to relocate to Europe and pursue a full-time jazz career. Of course, I was only lying to myself. I could never have any savings because of my addiction to gambling. During this time period, I could feel the Spirit of God wooing me to Himself. The desire to continue in my sinful lifestyle was diminishing, and likewise, the desire to know and serve God was becoming more urgent and intense!

Every payday, I would knock on the door of the paymaster of the hotel to receive my paycheck. His name was Clemen Sangrado. Clemen was different. He seemed to be overflowing with love, joy and peace (The Bible calls these the "fruit of The Spirit" in Galatians 5:22). In addition to his job at the hotel, Clemen was an evangelist and had a

ministry on the French side of the island. God was about to
use Clemen mightily in my life!

Clemen began to share with me his faith in Messiah
Yeshua. I began to tell him about myself, and my desire to
know and serve God. I told him that I was always searching
for truth and it seemed that God had been leading me to
put my faith in Messiah Yeshua. I told him I wasn't interested
in becoming religious but I wanted to know God personally. I
was 98% convinced that Yeshua was my Messiah but I needed
God to increase my faith. The Lord gave Clemen the words I
needed to hear. "God wants your commitment first, then
you will know Him." What God seemed to be saying to me
was: "It's not seeing is believing, but **believing is seeing!**"
The scripture states: " But without faith, it is impossible to
please Him, for He who comes to God must believe that He
is, and that He is a rewarder of those who diligently seek
Him." (Hebrews 11:6) At the same time God was convicting
me more and more of sin in my life and giving me more of a
desire to repent and get right with Him.

I had plans to stay in St. Maarten but God had other
plans for me. It probably was some time in late May 1979,
when the hotel gave me notice that they no longer would
need my services. Soon after, I was back on a plane headed
for New York City.

The Map

Soon after returning home, I went to visit with Elder
Hodelin of Rescue Church in Jamaica, Queens. I explained
that I believed in Yeshua 98% but I needed still more proof
to demonstrate that He indeed is the truth and our promised
Messiah. Elder Hodelin opened up the Bible to the Book of
Acts, chapter 2 and verse 36 where Peter states:
"Therefore, let the whole house of Israel know beyond doubt
that God had made him both Lord and Messiah- this Yeshua,
whom you executed on a stake!" (Jewish New Testament,

David H. Stern) "See, Jeff", Elder Hodelin said, "the Bible says in verse 36 that Yeshua is Lord and your Messiah." The thought came to my mind, "Yes, but can I believe that it's true just because the Bible says so?" God was about to use this wonderful man of God in a most profound way. The Lord knew what I needed to hear and Elder Hodelin was about to deliver the message! Baruch Ha Shem! He questioned me and asked: "If you were driving someplace and got lost, would you go to a gas station and ask the attendant for a map?" "Yes," was my immediate response. He then picked up his Bible and with an outstretched arm, made the gesture of handing it to me. "This is the map," he said with authority. The Lord used him to clarify my thinking. Prior to this, I would read the Bible as a wonderful book with a lot of truth. Now God assured me that the Bible was indeed God's infallible Word, and that I needed to receive it as such. The scriptures were no longer to be a smorgasbord of pithy sayings of which I had the option to pick and choose which sounded good to me and discard the rest. The Bible would now have the authority that God intended it to have in my life, the words of God penned by human authors. The Brit Hadasha (New Covenant) says in II Timothy 3:16: "All scripture is given by inspiration of God and is profitable for doctrine, for reproof, for correction, for instruction in righteousness." I Thessalonians 2:13 also bears witness of this very same spiritual truth and reality; it says: "When you received the Word of God, which you heard from us, you received it not as the word of men, but as it is in truth, the Word of God, which effectually works in you that believe." Finally the scripture says: "For the Word of God is living and powerful, and sharper than any two-edged sword, piercing even to the division of soul and spirit, and of joints and marrow, and is a discerner of the thoughts and intents of the heart." (Hebrews 4:12)

I had discovered that the Bible indeed was the map that would lead me to my long-awaited destination, the very presence of the living God of Israel. God had heard my prayers and was preparing my heart to receive Yeshua as my Messiah and Lord!

July 4, 1979- Independence Day!

It was the day before Independence Day, 1979. God had patiently and sovereignly answered all my questions concerning who He was and what He required of me. It was now my time to act. God was waiting for a decision and a response to his divine call! What a privilege! God, my heavenly Father, was always there, loving me and pointing me in the right direction, **His direction!** "The Lord is not slack concerning His promise, as some count slackness, but is longsuffering towards us, not willing that any should perish, but that all should come to repentance." (II Peter 3:9) It was time to make a 180- degree turnaround. The Bible says: "For godly sorrow works repentance to salvation not to be repented of, but the sorrow of the world works death." (II Corinthians 7:10) There are evidently two kinds of repentance, the godly kind and the ungodly, the acceptable and the unacceptable, the bogus and the genuine. God had given me His gift of godly sorrow so that I could repent and receive his salvation. I was tired of sin and saw the destructiveness of it in my own life. I acknowledged that it cost God the death of His Righteous One and only Son, Messiah Yeshua. I was tired of the emptiness of a life without God. I was tired of sin. I wanted God more than anything or anyone else in this world! I was ready to repent. I turned away from my sins and turned to God with all that was in me . I asked the Lord to forgive me of my sins and cleanse my heart and mind. I believed that Yeshua the Messiah died for my sins, and was buried and rose from the grave to justify me and give me eternal life. I made a commitment to serve God all the days of my life! I knew that I wouldn't have to do it on my own strength, but through

God's unlimited strength! I had just entered my room and lay on my bed. I asked the Lord one more thing. I hadn't had any rest or peace for as far back as I could remember. I asked the Lord to give me His peace and shalom and a good night's rest and sleep. The Holy Spirit spoke to my spirit reminding me of what King Messiah said in Matthew chapter 11 and verses 28-30: "Come to me, all you who labor and are heavy laden, and I will give you rest. Take my yoke upon you and learn from me, for I am gentle and lowly in heart, and you will find rest for your souls. For my yoke is easy and my burden is light." Suddenly, all burdens lifted! All guilt and condemnation due to sin left, and all confusion was gone! An incredible joy and peace flooded my heart, mind and soul!! I knew that God had forgiven me and "cast all my sins into the depth of the sea!" (Micah 7:19) I had been washed and cleansed by the shed blood of the eternal Lamb of God, Yeshua the Messiah! (I John 1:9) Immediately the power of God hit me; I was filled with the Ruach Elohim-the Spirit of God. I sensed His powerful presence and His boundless love! I was changed into another person! I knew that all of my sins had been forgiven. God had authenticated my belief with reality of the anointing of the Spirit of God. I had just had a powerful encounter with God! I now knew God **personally!** God had revealed Himself to me, **personally! Amazing!!!!** Not religion, but a vibrant **relationship!** This is what I always wanted, and what God desires for all of us. "If you seek me with all of your heart, **you will find me!"** (Jeremiah 29:13) It was July 4th, and I could hear the fireworks going off outside. But God had ignited a fire within me, and I was enjoying God's fireworks display in my heart. I understood what the prophet Jeremiah must have felt when he declared: "His word was in my heart like a burning fire, shut up in my bones!" (Jeremiah 20:9) It was Independence Day, independence from Satan, but total dependence on God from now on!

New Life in Messiah Yeshua!

I was brand new! "Therefore, if anyone is united with the Messiah, he is a new creation- the old has passed; look, what is come is fresh and new!" (II Corinthians 5:17 -The *Jewish New Testament*-David H. Stern-) I had received salvation and was "born from above" (John3:3.) I was given the gift of the Holy Spirit, and the Spirit bore witness with my spirit that I was a child of God. (Romans 8:16) I knew that I knew (that I knew) that if I were to die right then, I would spend eternity in God's presence. The weeks and months began to roll by and I noticed that I hadn't placed a bet. In fact, I had no desire to bet. God had taken the gambler out of me. I had been instantly cured, healed and delivered from my compulsive gambling addiction. **Amazing!!!** Gambler's Anonymous says "compulsive gambling is an illness that is progressive in nature and can **never be cured,** but can be arrested." This erroneous statement can be found on page 8 of a 17 page pamphlet printed by G.A. in March, 1994. Man says there is no known cure for compulsive gambling. God says; **"Therefore, if the Son makes you free, you shall be free indeed!!"** (John 8:36) "The things that are impossible with men **are possible with God!!!"** (Luke 18:27)

As I sit here at my computer keyboard typing this text, it is February, 2004. More than 24 years have passed since I came to know Messiah, and I haven't placed a bet or gambled, nor do I have any desire to do so. Today, I go to the racetrack to pray with people and share my testimony with them. I let them know what great things God has done for me, and what He can do for those who trust and obey Him! I was instantly delivered from compulsive gambling on Independence Day, 1979. I have a deep inner peace which the world didn't give to me! It comes from knowing Yeshua as my Messiah and Lord! The wisest wager I ever made was betting my life, on the nose, that Yeshua is the way, the truth and the life. What a hit!!! The largest payoff anyone could hope for; knowing God, being filled with His Spirit, receiving the forgiveness of sins, all guilt and condemnation gone, experiencing the love of God, receiving all of God's promises in His Word, having the peace of God that surpasses all human understanding, the ability to know God's voice and have the assurance of His presence with me and, oh yes, eternal life!!! What a spiritual fortune! What a great gift!! What a Great God we have!!! It reminds me of a song George Gershwin composed entitled: "I Got Rhythm." I would change one word of his lyrics and sing: "I got my **God,** who could ask for anything more!!" God has proven to me that He is faithful and keeps his covenant with those who love Him! He never changes! "Yeshua the Messiah is the same yesterday, today and forever." (Hebrews 13:8) God's promises are sure! What He has started in my life, He will complete! (Philippians 1:6) Whatever I have to go through in this life, He will use for my ultimate benefit to draw me closer to Him and fulfill His purposes in my life. (Romans 8:28)

The Truth about Compulsive Gambling

I would like to share with you some of the insights the Lord has shown me concerning compulsive gambling in light of spiritual truth. Compulsive gambling is a spiritual problem which has a spiritual solution. You must discard and reject the false diagnosis that compulsive gambling is a disease (as though you caught it like a cold) or an incurable illness. Compulsive gambling is a three letter word called **sin**. Sin means "missing the mark" and violates God's commandments and will for our lives. It results in receiving a curse rather than a blessing. God desires us to be good stewards of the material wealth which He has entrusted to us. It is to be used for blessing others and bringing glory to God. Compulsive gambling involves lying, covetousness, stealing, laziness and all sorts of irresponsible behavior which violate the commandments of God. This destructive life style will hurt others as well as yourself and is offensive to God. The gambler's life style is a form of idolatry. Yeshua says: "You cannot serve God and money." (Matthew 6:24) "The love of money (not money itself), is the root of all kinds of evil." (I Timothy 6:10)

Biblical truth applies to all people, of every nation. It applies to both the Jewish person and the non-Jew, the rich and poor alike, the addict, the "religious" individual, people in prisons, people of high estate, low estate and no estate, the serial killer and the "goody-two-shoes," the smoker and the non-smoker; it makes no difference, "for all have sinned and come short of the glory of God." (Romans 3:23) All people need to receive salvation from God which comes only through Yeshua the Messiah. There is a payoff for sin. "The wages of sin is death, but the gift of God is eternal life through Yeshua our Lord." (Romans 6:23). When we were born into this world, we were all born with an "evil inclination" or sinful nature, which we inherited from our first parents, Adam and Eve. This sin nature has a tremendous negative power over us. The sin nature can never be altered by self-denial, religion or philosophy. The good news is that the power of sin in our lives can be broken by the power of God, so that sin will no longer rule us. We no longer have to be slaves to the evil inclination and can be set free from its power and dominion in our lives! This was accomplished when Messiah died on a cross and rose again from the dead, defeating death, hell and Satan. When an individual puts his or her faith in the shed blood of Yeshua for personal atonement, **a miracle happens!** God comes into the individual's life in reality and power! You become "born again" by the Spirit of God. You experience God's forgiveness of sins as the Holy Spirit washes and cleanses your heart, mind and spirit. You are given a new heart and new mind by a **supernatural act of God.** You will then be empowered by HaShem to live a victorious life that is pleasing to God. You will be certain to inherit eternal life in the world to come. The overwhelming power that would literally force me to bet was demonic in origin. By continuing to serve sin, self and Satan, and having no fear of God, I unknowingly gave the devil more authority to try to destroy me. Demon spirits were deployed by Satan to wreak havoc in my life. Satan's plan was to keep me in bondage to sin and compulsive gambling while attempting to prevent me from knowing my Savior, Yeshua, the "light of the world!" In the end, I would spend an eternity without God and without hope in the presence of Satan and his demonic host. I'm glad that God has power over the enemy of our souls! God had another plan, a much better plan, a perfect plan which I am privileged to share with you.

I Was Born a Jew and I'll Die A Jew!

One thing I've always known is that I am a Jew by birth, and I will still be a Jew when God calls me home to be with Him! I was born a Jew and I'll die a Jew!! I've discovered that being Jewish is a great privilege and responsibility. I know that there is a difference between being a "secular Jew" and being a "biblical, spiritual Jew." The word Jew comes from the word Judah which means "praise." A true Jew is a "praiser of HaShem!" His or her life must bring praise and honor to the God of our fathers, to the God of Abraham, Isaac and Jacob, the God of Israel.

The greatest Jew who ever walked this earth according to the high moral and ethical mandates of Torah was Yeshua HaMashiach. **There is none His equal!** When He was asked by some scribes what is the greatest and first commandment (recorded in the gospel of Mark 12:28), Yeshua replied: "The first of all the commandments is: Hear O Israel, the Lord our God, the Lord is one." He quoted the "Sh'ma," the foundational declaration of the Jewish faith and the faith of the patriarchs found in the Torah, Deuteronomy 6:4. Yeshua continues: "And you shall love the Lord your God with all your heart, with all your soul, with all your mind, and with all your strength: this is the first commandment. And the second, like it, is this: You shall love your neighbor as yourself. There is no other commandment greater than these." Yeshua's mission as King Messiah, was to live a perfect and sinless life motivated by divine love. He lived out Torah to its fullest expression of righteousness, never once breaking any of God's commandments. Yeshua is the very goal at which the Torah aims! Yeshua was empowered by HaShem to work miracles never seen on this earth, which authenticated that He was indeed the Son of God, King Messiah and the Savior of the world!! Yeshua was willing to accept the penalty for our sins and our violation of Torah, which was death. He became the only perfect sacrifice acceptable to God for atonement of our sins. He willingly suffered and died a horrible death on a Roman cross in our place, so that we could receive forgiveness of sins and eternal life and be empowered by God's Spirit to live out Torah! God raised Yeshua from the dead, and now Yeshua is seated in God's Glory throne room as our Great High Priest (*Cohen HaGadol*), living forever to make intercession for us. He will one day return to *eretz Yisrael* (the land of Israel) to reign as King Messiah from Jerusaslem. The *Tanakh* declares that Yeshua is indeed our promised Messiah. Yeshua said to His Jewish brethren: "You keep examining the *Tanakh* because you think that in it you have eternal life. Those very scriptures bear witness to me, but you won't come to me in order to have life!" (John 5:39-40, *The Jewish New Testament*-David H. Stern) As a Jew, I follow Torah and love the God of my fathers, the God of Abraham, Isaac and Jacob, the only true and living God. True biblical apostolic Christianity is nothing less than Torah-apocalyptic Judaism. I love the rich heritage of our Jewish people. Since Yeshua is our Jewish Messiah, there's nothing more Jewish than to believe in Him and follow all of His teachings. I was born a Jew and I'll die a Jew! I am certain that when God calls me home, I will spend eternity with Him just as He has promised me in His

Word! He never fails; He's faithful and worthy of all our trust; what He says He will do; He does. He has both the power and the authority to do whatever He says He'll do. You can bank on it! **He never fails!!!**

The Last and Final Bet - Post Time is Coming for You

Every horse player knows about post time. This is when the horses are gathered in the starting gate, and the race is about to be run. It is the time of reckoning. All eyes and ears are focused on the horses and on the announcer's voice calling the race. The race is about to start, and the way a horse runs the race will determine how he finishes. Life is just like that. Life is like a race (New Yorkers can instantly relate to this!) The Bible says to "lay aside every weight and the sin which so easily ensnares us, and let us **run with endurance the race that is set before us**, looking unto Yeshua, the author and finisher of our faith, who for the joy that was set before Him endured the cross, despising the shame, and has sat down at the right hand of the throne of God."(Hebrews 12:1-2) Post time is coming for all of us. We will all stand before Almighty God, the righteous judge, and give an account to Him for all of our actions and deeds, thoughts and motives. We will be responsible for acting or not acting upon the light He has graciously shown us. God's Word, the Bible, tells us how to run a good race, stand before Him justified and uncondemned, be a winner, and enter into His presence forever. I liken post time to God reviewing the videotape of our lives. How did we run this race? How did we finish? This race will end when we breathe our last breath, and then the Lord will post the official result. Death is certain for all of us. We might avoid taxes, but we can't avoid death. "It is appointed for men to die once, but after this the judgment." (Hebrews 9:27) Tomorrow isn't promised to anyone, and you do not know when God will call you to the post! Evangelist and author Steven Hill once said that: "tomorrow is a day in a fool's calendar!" The Word of God declares: "Today, if you will hear His voice, do not harden your hearts." (Hebrews 4:7) We have got to be prepared and ready for the day of our departure from this life this very day! I do firmly believe that if we aren't ready to be with the Lord, we will never experience the fullness of life as God intended it to be. Every gambler likes to bet on a horse that has shown some consistency. Why not check out Messiah Yeshua's track record? He's never failed a trusting heart! If you bet on Yeshua, you can't lose!! At the racetrack, there is win, place and show betting on most races, but in God's economy, there is win betting only. There are two entries, God and the devil. God was and always will be the victor! You might say: "I'm not interested. I don't want to get involved in betting on this race." Well, my friend, whether you know it or not, you are already very much involved. There is a spiritual battle going on in your life concerning the salvation of your soul. You have a very real enemy, who is Satan. God has been warring against him on your behalf, but your victory or defeat will be based on your true heart-felt commitment and decision whether or not to trust Yeshua as your Messiah, Savior and Lord. The Word of God declares that if, for any reason, you do not trust God with all of your heart and bet your life to win on Messiah Yeshua, you have, in effect, bet on the losing entry, who is Satan. Satan was eternally defeated when Messiah rose from the dead. By rejecting the truth of God's message, God's mercy and God's love, you, too, will be eternally defeated and your *nefesh*(soul) will be eternally lost and separated from the love and presence of your heavenly Father forever. The Word declares that people will be lost because they, "did not receive the **love of the truth**, that they might be saved. And for this reason God will send them strong delusion, that they should believe the lie, that they all may be condemned who did not believe the truth but had pleasure in unrighteousness. (II Thessalonians 2:10-12). Post time is certainly coming my friend. Don't be a fool and do nothing about it! Right now, step up to God's twenty-four hour betting window and by faith, bet your very life on Messiah on the nose! (to win!) Repent and turn away from sin and your sinful lifestyle and turn to the God of Israel **right now**. Believe the good news that Yeshua is indeed your promised Messiah. Believe in your heart that He suffered and died a cruel death for your sins so you could receive atonement and forgiveness. Believe in your heart that God raised Him from the dead, and He now is seated at the right hand of the throne of God. Personally invite Messiah to come into your heart and save you from your sins and ask Him to be Lord of your life. God is faithful to His Word and will always honor a trusting and sincere heart. Post time is surely coming for **you!**

It is Now Post Time

"Then I saw a great white throne, and Him who sat on it, from whose face the earth and the heaven fled away. And there was found no place for them. And I saw the dead, small and great, standing before God and the books were opened. And another book was opened, which is the Book of Life. And the dead were judged according to their works by the things which were written in the books. The sea gave up the dead who were in it, and Death and Hades delivered up the dead who were in them. And they were judged, each one according to his works. Then Death and Hades were cast into the lake of fire. This is the second death. And anyone not found written in the Book of Life was cast into the lake of fire." (Revelation 20:11-15)

Yeshua tells us what happens after we die. "Once there was a rich man who used to dress in the most expensive clothing and spent his days in magnificent luxury. At his gate had been laid a beggar named El'azar who was covered with sores. He would have been glad to eat the scraps that fell from the rich man's table; but instead, even the dogs would come and lick his sores. In time the beggar died and was carried away by the angels to Avraham's side; the rich man also died and was buried. In *Sh'ol* [hades, hell], where he was in torment, the rich man looked up and saw Avraham far away with El'azar at his side. He called out, "Father Avraham, take pity on me, and send El'azar just to dip the tip of his finger in water to cool my tongue, because I'm in agony in this fire!' However, Avraham said, 'Son, **remember** that when you were alive, you got the good things while he got the bad; but now he gets his consolation here, while you are the one in agony. Yet that isn't all: between you and us a deep rift has been established, so that those who would like to pass from here to you cannot, nor can anyone cross over from there to us.' He answered, 'Then, father, I beg you to send him to my father's house, where I have five brothers, to warn them; so that they may be spared having to come to this place of torment too.' But Avraham said, 'They have Moshe and the Prophets; they should listen to them.' However, he said, 'No, father Avraham, they need more. If someone from the dead goes to them, they'll repent!' But he replied, 'If they won't listen to Moshe and the Prophets, they won't be convinced even if someone rises from the dead!'" (Recorded in the Gospel of Luke, chapter 16, verses 19-31.) **

Won't you listen to Moshe and the prophets???

Yeshua is God's choice! I'm hoping that you will make Him yours!!

**Scripture quotations are taken from the Jewish New Testament, copyright 1979 by David H. Stern and used with permission of Jewish New Testament Publications, Inc., P.O Box 615, Clarksville, Maryland 21029. Available through Messianic Jewish Resources.
www.messianicjewish.net